Contents

What are wheel sports?

Wheel sports are sports that involve vehicles that you can ride on or drive. Some of these vehicles use your **energy** to power them, while others are powered by engines.

EXTREME SPORT

WHEEL SPORTS

Michael Hurley

www.raintreepublishers.co.uk
Visit our website to find out
more information about
Raintree books.

To order:

☎ Phone 0845 6044371

🖹 Fax +44 (0) 1865 312263

🖵 Email myorders@raintreepublishers.co.uk

Customers from outside the UK please telephone +44 1865 312262

Raintree is an imprint of Capstone Global Library
Limited, a company incorporated in England and
Wales having its registered office at 7 Pilgrim Street,
London, EC4V 6LB – Registered company number:
6695582

Text © Capstone Global Library Limited 2012
First published in hardback in 2012
The moral rights of the proprietor have been
asserted.

Edited by Rebecca Rissman, Dan Nunn, and
Catherine Veitch
Designed by Joanna Hinton Malivoire
Picture research by Ruth Blair
Originated by Capstone Global Library
Printed and bound in China by CTPS

ISBN 978 1 406 22695 9
15 14 13 12 11
10 9 8 7 6 5 4 3 2 1

British Library Cataloguing in Publication Data
Hurley, Michael
Wheel sports. – (Extreme sport)
796.6-dc22
A full catalogue record for this book is available
from the British Library.

Acknowledgements
We would like to thank the following for permission
to reproduce photographs: Alamy pp. 10
(© ClassicStock), 26 (© StockShot); Corbis pp. 5
(© FRANCK ROBICHON/epa), 9 (© Troy Wayrynen/
NewSport), 11 (© Radius Images), 16 (© GEOFF
CADDICK/epa), 17 (© Lubomir Asenov/epa), 20
(© Floris Leeuwenberg/The Cover Story), 21 (©
Patrick Seeger/epa), 24 (© Reuters); Getty Images
pp. 13 (Stefan Postles/Stringer), 15 (Rapsodia), 14
(Tom Hauck), 25 (AFP); PA Photos p. 23 (Sutton);
Shutterstock p. 4 (© Ljupco Smokovski), 6 (© Iakov
Filimonov), 7 (© A & B Photos), 8 (© Timothy Large),
12 (© dmvphotos), 18 (© Walter G Arce), 19 (©
Walter G Arce), 22 (© Sillycoke), 27 (© Stanislav
Fridkin), 28 (© Monkey Business Images), 29
(© Aturner).

Cover photograph of motocross reproduced with
permission of Corbis (© Richard Hamilton Smith).

Every effort has been made to contact copyright
holders of material reproduced in this book. Any
omissions will be rectified in subsequent printings if
notice is given to the publisher.

All the internet addresses (URLs) given in this book
were valid at the time of going to press. However,
due to the dynamic nature of the internet, some
addresses may have changed, or sites may have
changed or ceased to exist since publication. While
the author and publisher regret any inconvenience
this may cause readers, no responsibility for any
such changes can be accepted by either the
author or the publisher.

Some words are shown in bold, **like this**. You can find
out what they mean by looking in the glossary.

helmet

glove

padded suit

strong boot

Wheel sports can be dangerous. To enjoy some extreme wheel sports you need special **equipment** and **protective** clothing.

!

STAY SAFE!

Remember that safety is important. Look on page 26 to see how you can stay safe while enjoying wheel sports.

BMX racing

In BMX, or bicycle motocross racing, riders battle against each other over a short, fast track with bumps, bends, and straights. The riders wear **protective** clothing: a helmet, gloves, and padding.

WOW!

BMX biking first took place in California, USA, in the 1960s. BMX racing has been included in the Olympics since 2008.

Mountain biking

Mountain biking began around the same time as BMX biking. People started taking their bikes "**off road**" along mountain trails. New bikes were specially designed and built to make off road riding more comfortable.

New mountain bike sports have been created over the years. There are **competitive** races such as downhill and cross-country racing. Other competitions include dirt jumping and street riding.

WOW!
Mountain bikers call the lowest **gear** on a mountain bike the "Granny Gear"!

Street luge

Street luge is a very dangerous sport. It developed from skateboarding. Street lugers lie flat on their boards and race downhill. Street luges have up to six wheels and are 2.5 metres long (longer than an adult).

helmet

padded leather suit

WOW!

Street luges can travel up to 100 kilometres an hour. That's as fast as a car on a motorway!

Formula 1

Formula 1 is the highest level of motor sport in the world. The best drivers in the world drive in Formula 1. They drive specially designed cars.

WOW!
A Formula 1 car can cost up to 200 million pounds!

Formula 1 cars can travel faster than 300 kilometres an hour. **Spectators** love the speed of racing.

NASCAR

NASCAR stands for National Association for Stock Car Auto Racing. Most NASCAR races are held on oval tracks. The cars only ever turn left during the race! NASCAR is the most popular **spectator** sport in the United States.

WOW!
NASCAR cars can reach speeds of almost 322 kilometres an hour.

Inline skating

Inline skates have been around since the 1700s. Today there are many types of inline skating that all involve performing tricks and jumps.

WOW!

Frenchman Jean-Yves Blondeau has created a body suit out of inline skates. He calls it a Buggy-Rollin. He can travel at speeds of up to 120 kilometres an hour. That's as fast as a cheetah!

Karting

If you like fast racing cars then you might like to try karting. Indoor karts can reach speeds of up to 64 kilometres an hour. Outdoor karts usually travel up to 129 kilometres an hour.

WOW!

Formula 1 driver Lewis Hamilton started out in kart racing.

Freestyle motocross

Freestyle motocross is an exciting and dangerous motorbike sport. Riders **accelerate** up a mound and jump at the top. While they are in the air they perform tricks. Points are awarded for skill and **technique**.

WOW!

Australian freestyle rider Robbie Maddison jumped his bike over the Corinth Canal in Greece in 2010.

Be safe!

When you are taking part in wheel sports it is important to be safe. You should always wear the proper **equipment**. Make sure you listen to **experts** and have many lessons.

An adult should always be with you
if you are going to take part in any
extreme sports.

Get fit!

Most wheel sports require strength and **stamina**. To help you build up your stamina you can perform exercises like sit ups.

To do a sit up you need to lie on your back and then bring your head as close to your knees as you can. Relax, and then repeat this movement. Keep repeating it until you are tired out!

Glossary

accelerate go faster

competitive trying to do something better than someone else

energy strength or power to work or be active

equipment tools or clothing that you need

expert person with a special skill or knowledge

freestyle event in which competitors can use any style they wish

gear changes the speed of a machine

off road not sticking to a road or path

protective something that stops you from being harmed or injured

spectator person who goes to watch a sport

stamina strength that allows someone to do something for a long time

technique way of doing something

Find out more

Books

Motorsports: Formula 1, Clive Gifford
(Franklin Watts, 2009)

Motorsports: Karting, Clive Gifford
(Franklin Watts, 2009)

To the Extreme: Mountain Biking, Sarah L. Schuette
(Capstone, 2005)

World Sports Guide: BMX and Mountain Biking,
Paul Mason (A & C Black, 2010)

Websites

http://readyforten.com/skills/16-bmx
This site has a few ideas about improving your
BMX skills.

**www.bbc.co.uk/northernireland/schools/4_11/
uptoyou/**
This website has lots of information about healthy
eating and exercise. Why not get fit and enjoy
those extreme sports?

Index